If you would be a practiser of limning mark this.
Cleanliness is therefore fittest for a gentleman and
if you would limn be precisely pure and clean
in your doings. Grind only the finest of pigments
and in a place where there is neither dust nor smoke.
May your apparel at the least be silk such as
sheddeth the least dust or hairs. Touch not your
work with the fingers nor with any hard thing
and brush it not clean save with a white feather.
Take heed of the shedding of the dandruff
from the hair and neither breathe on your work
and desist from speaking over it for sparkling
of spittle will never be helped if it light in the face
or any part of the picture. Work only in a room
where neither dust, smoke, noise nor stench may
offend for a good limner hath tender senses,
quiet and apt.

A Gentleman

Is she kind as she is fair?
For beauty lives with kindness:
Love doth to her eyes repair,
To help him of his blindness;
And, being help'd inhabits there.

To me fair friend, you can never be old,
For as you were when first your eye I ey'd,
Such seems your beauty still.

Take, O take those lips away,
That so sweetly were forsworn;
And those eyes, the break of day,
Lights that do mislead the morn;

My bounty is as boundless as the sea,
My love as deep: the more I give to thee,
The more I have, for both are infinite.

Thou for whom e'en Jove would swear
Juno but an Ethiop were;
And deny himself for Jove,
Turning mortal for thy love.

If music be the food of love, play on;
  Give me excess of it, that, surfeiting,
  The appetite may sicken, and so die.
  That strain again! it had a dying fall;
O! it came o'er my ear like the sweet sound
  That breathes upon a bank of violets,
      Stealing and giving odour!
        Enough! no more:
  'Tis not so sweet now as it was before.

In Belmont is a lady richly left,
And she is fair, and fairer than the word,
Of wondrous virtues; sometimes from her eyes
I did receive fair speechless messages.

You would play upon me;
You would seem to know my stops;
You would pluck out the heart of my mystery;
You would sound me from my lowest note
to the top of my compass.

O! know, sweet love, I always write of you,
And you and love are still my argument;
So all my best is dressing old words new,
Spending again what is already spent.

Being your slave,
what should I do but tend
Upon the hours and times of your desire?
I have no precious time at all to spend,
Nor services to do, till you require.

O! she doth teach the torches to burn bright,
It seems she hangs upon the cheek of night
Like a rich jewel in an Ethiop's ear:
Beauty too rich for use, for earth too dear.

It was a lover and his lass,
With a hey, and a ho, and a hey nonino,
That o'er the green cornfield did pass,
In the spring time, the only pretty ring time,
When birds do sing, hey ding a ding, ding;
Sweet lovers love the spring.

Live with me and be my love,
And we will all the pleasures prove,
That hills and valleys, dales and fields,
And all the craggy mountains yeilds.

What is love? 'tis not hereafter;
Present mirth hath present laughter;
What's to come is still unsure;
In delay there lies no plenty;
Then come kiss me, sweet and twenty,
Youth's a stuff will not endure.

If I could write the beauty of your eyes
And in fresh numbers number all your graces,
The age to come would say, 'This poet lies;
Such heavenly touches ne'er touch'd earthly faces.'
So should my papers, yellow'd with their age,
Be scorn'd, like old men of less truth than tongue,
And your true rights be term'd a poet's rage
And stretched metre of an antique song.

O! how this spring of love resembleth
The uncertain glory of an April day,
Which now shows all the beauty of the sun,
And by and by a cloud takes all away!

Hark! hark! the lark at
heaven's gate sings,
And Phoebus 'gins arise,
His steeds to water at those springs
On chalic'd flowers that lies;
And winking Mary-buds begin
To ope their golden eyes:
With everything that pretty is,
My lady sweet, arise!

*Your eyes are lodestars!
and your tongue's sweet air
More tuneable than lark to shepherds ear,
When wheat is green, when hawthorn
buds appear.*

From fairest creatures we desire increase,
That thereby beauty's rose might never die:

Say that she rail; why then I'll tell her plain
She sings as sweetly as a nightingale;
Say that she frown; I'll say she looks as clear
As morning roses newly wash'd with dew;
Say she be mute and will not speak a word;
Then I'll commend her volubility,
And say she uttereth piercing eloquence.

Tell me where is fancy bred,
Or in the heart or in the head?
How begot, how nourished?
Reply, reply.

It is engender'd in the eyes,
With gazing fed; and fancy dies
In the cradle where it lies.
Let us all ring fancy's knell:
I'll begin it, - Ding, dong, bell.

Shall I compare thee to a summer's day?
Thou art more lovely and more temperate:
Rough winds do shake the darling buds of May,
And summer's lease hath all too short a date: